Who Is
Colin Kaepernick?

Who Is Colin Kaepernick?

by Lakita Wilson

illustrated by Gregory Copeland

Penguin Workshop

For my brothers, LRW and CAWIII,
who love football, and who I hope will
always "Know Your Rights"—LW

PENGUIN WORKSHOP
An imprint of Penguin Random House LLC, New York

First published in the United States of America by Penguin Workshop,
an imprint of Penguin Random House LLC, New York, 2022

Visit us online at penguinrandomhouse.com.

Library of Congress Cataloging-in-Publication Data is available.

Printed in the United States of America

ISBN 9780593519400 (paperback)   10 9 8 7 6 5 4 3 2 1 WOR
ISBN 9780593519417 (library binding)   10 9 8 7 6 5 4 3 2 1 WOR

Contents

Alton Sterling

Philando Castile

Who Is Colin Kaepernick?

As the United States national anthem began playing on August 14, 2016, professional football player Colin Kaepernick remained seated on the bench while his teammates stood and placed their hands over their hearts.

Although it is tradition, it's not a requirement to play the national anthem before sporting events. Playing it has long been considered a way for United States citizens to show their respect and love for their country. However, Colin Kaepernick didn't feel much love or respect for his country in that moment. A month earlier, two Black men—Alton Sterling and Philando Castile—had been unfairly targeted and killed by police officers in Minnesota and Louisiana. And no officers were ever found guilty of committing a crime.

Colin refused to stand for the pregame playing of the national anthem again on August 20 for the same reason. However, no one noticed Colin sitting out because he wasn't wearing his football uniform. He had been injured and wasn't going to play in the first two preseason games.

Things changed on August 26, 2016. Colin was due to play for the first time that season against the Green Bay Packers and had suited up in his game jersey. While the anthem played, Colin sat on the bench. A reporter named Jennifer Lee Chan tweeted out a photo of the football field during the anthem. Twitter users noticed Colin Kaepernick sitting on the bench. During the game, social media users all over the country wondered why Colin remained seated. After the game, Colin told reporters that he remained seated "to protest the injustices that are happening in America."

Two days later, Colin gave more details during another interview with the press, where he explained that his protest was about giving a voice to people who weren't being heard. He said people were dying because the United States wasn't keeping their promise to provide freedom, justice, and liberty to all, citing the experiences of Black people. He told the media—and the world—that until he saw change, he would not stand up for the national anthem.

Many people became angry with Colin's decision to sit out during the national anthem. They felt like Colin was disrespecting the American flag, the country, and the soldiers who fought for the country and the American people.

Colin said this wasn't true. He said that he respected the American soldiers.

Colin ended his speech by saying he wouldn't

stop protesting until police brutality ends. "I am not going to stand up to show pride in a flag for a country that oppresses Black people and people of color."

On August 30, Nate Boyer, a former soldier from the Green Beret unit of the United States Army, wrote Colin Kaepernick an open letter— a letter that is not private but available for the public to read as well. In Nate's letter, he told Colin that although he was initially upset when the San Francisco 49ers quarterback sat during the anthem, he is now trying to listen and understand. In a later meeting with Colin, Nate offered a better way to protest, without disrespecting the soldiers. He said that soldiers take a knee in front of their fallen brothers' graves to show respect. Colin agreed to compromise and protest this way.

In the final preseason game on September 1, 2016, Colin suited up in his football uniform to play against the San Diego Chargers. Colin Kaepernick, along with his teammate defensive back Eric Reid, took a knee while the national anthem played.

Eric Reid and Colin Kaepernick

CHAPTER 1
A Kid Named Kap

Colin Kaepernick was born on November 3, 1987, in Milwaukee, Wisconsin. Colin's birth father had left shortly after his birth mother became pregnant with Colin. Colin's birth mother, nineteen-year-old Heidi, didn't know how she would be able to take care of a new baby. So Heidi placed Colin up for adoption when he was five weeks old. A few towns over, in Fond du Lac, Wisconsin, a couple were looking to adopt a baby.

Rick and Teresa Kaepernick already had a son and a daughter. But their last two sons had died shortly after birth. After grieving, Rick and Teresa decided to adopt their next baby. When they met Colin, the couple fell in love and brought him home to live with them. Teresa called Colin her "perfect child."

But everything wasn't perfect. Rick, Teresa, and their birth children were all white. Colin was biracial; his birth mother was white, and his birth father was Black. Having a different skin color than other family members can be difficult for kids who are a different race than their adoptive family. But Colin's parents discussed his adoption with him early on. They frequently reminded their young son that his darker skin color reflected both his African American and white heritage— all the parts of his background that made him Colin.

Rick and Teresa never treated Colin like he was white. They acknowledged his mixed-race background and made sure they listened to his requests for things that honored his Black heritage.

When Colin was four years old, the Kaepernick

Colin with his older adoptive siblings

family moved to Turlock, California. In Fond du Lac, almost everyone had been white. Although more races were represented in Turlock, most of the people were still white. It was in this new town that Colin and his family began experiencing racism—or mistreatment based on a person's race or ethnic group—from their neighbors and strangers. When playmates saw Colin's brown skin compared to his parents' white skin, they would ask, "Who's your real mother?" Children *and* adults sometimes stared as Colin walked alongside his family.

After Colin showed an interest and natural talent in sports, Teresa and Rick Kaepernick signed him up for football when he was eight years old. Colin played as a defensive end and punter. At nine, his skills earned him the quarterback position on his youth league team. During football's offseason, Colin also played Little League baseball. He played baseball just as well as he played football. So well that white parents often grumbled from the stands, making racist comments about the "Black kid" striking out their sons. When Colin's mother heard their racist remarks, she made sure to call them out on their hate speech.

Although Colin was a great baseball player, football was his first love. When he was in fourth

Dear San Fransisco 49ers,

Colin Kaepernick
Turlock CA 95380

I'm 5ft 2inches 91 pounds. Good N athel-t.
I think in 7 years I will be between
6ft - to 6ft 4inches. 110 pounds, I hope
Then go to a good college in football
on the go to the pro pros and play
they niners or the packers even if
My wernt good in seven years.
Spencer, Mark and Jacob

insisco 49ers
estick Park
S Town Ave. CA
Fransisco 94124

Sincerly
Colin

grade at Dutcher Elementary School, he even wrote a letter predicting he would someday play for one of his dream teams, the San Francisco 49ers.

CHAPTER 2
Destined for the 49ers

At John H. Pitman High School, Colin continued playing multiple sports. By his senior year, he was nominated for all-state in football, basketball, and baseball. And even though Colin was mostly known for his baseball skills, winning many awards as his school's all-star pitcher, he continued hoping that someday he'd be able to play football professionally.

By his senior year of high school, Colin was already six feet, four inches tall but only weighed 170 pounds. This worried his high-school football coaches. They thought he was much too thin for such an aggressive sport. They kept him from running the ball to limit his chances of injury. But this also meant college recruiters didn't get many chances to see him play.

Pitman High's head football coach, Larry Nigro, had made a highlight tape of Colin's best moves on the football field during his junior year. Colin's brother, Kyle, made copies of this tape and sent it out to one hundred Division 1—or highest level—college football programs. Some of those schools showed interest in Colin, but none of the schools offered him a football scholarship.

The baseball scholarships, however, were rolling in. Several colleges offered Colin a full ride to play baseball for them, but Colin desperately wanted his shot to play football. Then the unbelievable happened. An assistant football coach at the University of Nevada, Reno, saw Colin dominate a high-school basketball game on a night where he was running a 102 degree fever! Impressed with Colin's speed, the assistant coach convinced Nevada's head football coach to offer Colin scholarship money.

Colin accepted his only football scholarship and headed to the University of Nevada, Reno, in 2006. Although recruited to play safety, the coaches decided to redshirt Colin—this means they had him sit out the first season to work on

his skills and prepare for the upcoming season. However, during the fifth game of his next season, the head coach called Colin in to replace the injured quarterback. Colin played so well, he continued to play for the rest of the season.

Colin led the Nevada Wolf Pack to victory often as the college's star quarterback. By Colin's senior year, everyone around him predicted he would surely play in the National Football League (NFL). On April 29, 2011, in the second round of the NFL Draft, the San Francisco 49ers picked Colin Kaepernick to play for their team.

Colin served as backup quarterback during his rookie season with the 49ers. But during the next season, in 2012, the team's longtime quarterback Alex Smith suffered a head injury and Colin took over. On November 19, 2012, Colin Kaepernick started the game as the team's quarterback for the first time. His fourth-grade dream had finally come true. Colin used his speed and arm strength to lead his team to victory against the Chicago Bears. The 49ers head coach, Jim Harbaugh, was impressed. After the 49ers won several games with Colin leading the way, Jim had to make a tough decision. Would he put Alex Smith back in the game or would he continue letting his talented new quarterback start? In the end, Jim decided that Colin's speed and arm strength made him the best man for the starting position and made Colin the permanent starting quarterback for the rest of the season.

With Colin leading the team, the 49ers scored big in the playoffs and made it all the way to the Super Bowl, where they lost to the Baltimore Ravens. Colin was disappointed. But even though Colin lost the Super Bowl, he had won something else: respect in the eyes of his teammates, his coaches, and football fans all over the country. Colin Kaepernick was a rising star.

After making it to the Super Bowl in the 2012–2013 season, Colin returned to the field the next season determined to win a Super Bowl ring.

But this time the 49ers didn't make it to the Super Bowl at all. They lost their chance in the playoffs, losing to the Seattle Seahawks.

Colin starts for the San Francisco 49ers

Colin continued playing well, but sports injuries led to surgeries on his thumb, knee, and shoulder, which slowed him down.

By early 2016, Colin felt his best chance at winning a Super Bowl ring would be on another team. He asked to be traded.

CHAPTER 3
Fed Up with Injustice

The summer of 2016 was devastating to the Black community. Police officers in Louisiana and Minnesota were responsible for the deaths of two unarmed Black men, Alton Sterling and Philando Castile. Plenty of Black people had been victim to senseless police brutality before, but this time, the murders happened one day apart. None of the officers involved in these deaths were found guilty of committing any crimes.

Like many Black Americans, Colin Kaepernick was fed up with the injustice of no one being held responsible for these murders. He wanted to see change. Unfortunately, Alton, Philando, and countless other victims could not speak up for themselves. The families of the victims weren't being heard, either. Many people in the Black community also wanted change, but they didn't have large audiences to hear their voices.

But Colin had stadiums full of football fans. His protests against these injustices could be broadcast to millions of people who watched professional football each week. Colin decided that he would use his platform to speak for all those who wanted to fight back.

During Colin's final preseason football game, he and one of his teammates, safety Eric Reid, took a knee together to show they were fed up about the murders of Black people by police officers and would not stand for the national anthem until they saw change.

By now, football fans knew about Colin's protests. Many people felt what Colin was doing was unpatriotic—that he was not showing love for his country.

After the anthem, football fans at the stadium chanted, "U-S-A! U-S-A!"

Two fans showed off a sign with the message "You're an American. Start acting like one."

Despite the backlash toward Colin, he had support from some of his teammates. Other Black football players started kneeling, too. Minutes after Colin and Eric took a knee, Seattle Seahawks cornerback Jeremy Lane sat on the bench at his own football game against the Oakland Raiders. The following week, Denver Broncos linebacker Brandon Marshall took a knee at his first regular season game on September 8. Two sponsors stopped working with Brandon because of this, but he didn't care. He, like Colin, cared more about justice for Black people than the sponsorship money he was losing.

By this time, important people in and outside of the football community had the opportunity to weigh in. NFL commissioner Roger Goodell, speaking about Colin, told the Associated Press, "I don't necessarily agree with what he is doing."

But the president of the United States thought differently. President Barack Obama defended Colin, saying, "He cares about some real, legitimate issues that need to be talked about."

On September 11, 2016, the US national anthem would have more meaning than usual. September 11 is the anniversary of the terrorist attack on the Twin Towers in New York City and the Pentagon building just outside of Washington, DC. Four Miami Dolphins players stood for the 9/11 acknowledgement in memory of the many Americans who lost their lives in 2001, but they still took a knee during the national anthem.

On September 12, Colin and Eric took a knee again. This time, other members of their team stood but raised their fists high in the air— the Black Power salute—to show Colin they supported his protest. Even members of the opposing team raised their fists. And professional athletes weren't the only ones kneeling for justice. High-school football players, college cheerleaders, and middle-school and high-school band members were also taking a knee.

That fall, more and more Black NFL players across the country took a knee during the national anthem in support of Colin and justice for Black people. The National Basketball Association (NBA), Women's National Basketball Association (WNBA), and professional soccer players joined them. Celebrities like NBA player Iman Shumpert pledged money for the cause. "I'm with Kap" became a popular phrase to say or tweet to show support for Colin Kaepernick's protest.

"Once again, I'm not anti-American," Kaepernick said in a 2016 interview. "I love America. I love people. That's why I'm doing this. I want to help make America better."

Colin backed up his words with action by founding the Know Your Rights Camp to help educate Black and Brown kids, who are more likely to face injustice or brutality from police officers. His partner, Nessa Diab, and a few friends pitched in. On September 29, 2016, dressed in a black T-shirt that featured the words I KNOW MY RIGHTS across the chest, Colin held his first camp session in Oakland, California.

He talked to hundreds of kids about how to interact with the police safely. He explained that learning about police violence, education, financial literacy, and nutrition were all ways kids could fight back against oppression—or continuous cruel and unjust treatment—in this country. Colin also helped children understand their rights as United States citizens. At the end of his session, each kid received their own T-shirt with a list of ten points on the back, to remind them they were worthy of health,

safety, love, and freedom.

By the end of September, twenty-eight-year-old Colin Kaepernick appeared on the cover of *TIME* magazine, taking a knee in his 49ers football uniform. Popular sports channel ESPN reported that Colin had been voted the "most disliked" player in the NFL. Around 29 percent of football fans voted "disliked a lot" under Colin's name. Two years before he began protesting, only 6 percent of football fans voted against him. Despite the criticism, Colin's team jersey became a top seller and sold out of stores everywhere.

On January 1, 2017, Colin Kaepernick played his last NFL game of the 2016–2017 season. On March 3, 2017, Colin decided to opt out of his contract, making him a free agent— or someone who isn't on a team but can be recruited by any team that wants them.

No teams asked Colin to join them for the

2017 NFL season. This meant Colin was without a team and without a job. He couldn't play the game he loved and didn't have a field to kneel on. But players from every NFL team supported him anyway. When the 2017 season began, more players than ever took a knee during the national anthem.

"If they take football away, my endorsements from me," he said, "I know that I stood up for what is right."

CHAPTER 4
Time for Change

By the 2017 NFL season, a new president of the United States of America had been elected. This new president had a slogan that claimed he would work hard to "Make America Great Again." Unfortunately, President Donald Trump didn't think justice for Black people was a part of making America great. Instead of focusing on why Colin and the other NFL players were kneeling during the national anthem, he chose to attack them.

At a rally in Alabama on September 22, 2017, Donald Trump gave a speech to the crowd that urged NFL team owners to fire any football player who refused to stand for the national anthem.

Football owners weren't firing players for kneeling. But they weren't hiring the person who began the protest, Colin Kaepernick, either. On October 15, 2017, Colin filed an official complaint against NFL owners. In the legal paperwork, he accused the owners of working together to make sure he was blackballed—or prevented—from playing football professionally. Colin felt he was being punished for protesting racist acts in the United States.

Colin Kaepernick may have been out of a job in the NFL, but he was being celebrated all over the country for his activism. A month after Colin filed his complaint to the NFL, *Sports Illustrated* magazine named Colin as the recipient of the Muhammad Ali Legacy Award. This honor is only given to past athletes who have shown a great deal of sportsmanship, leadership, and philanthropy (promoting and donating to good causes) to help change the world.

GQ magazine released its December issue with Colin on the cover. They named him *GQ*'s Citizen of the Year. On December 4, 2017, the world learned that Colin was a finalist for *TIME* magazine's Person of the Year.

The following year, in May 2018, NFL owners approved a new rule banning players from kneeling during the national anthem. They told players if they wanted to protest, they could remain in the locker room. But any player on the field must stand for the anthem.

This new rule sparked such outrage with the players and the public, the NFL never enforced it and players continued to kneel.

Then, on September 3, 2018, the shoe-and-sports-apparel company Nike revealed Colin Kaepernick as the face of their "Just Do It" thirtieth-anniversary campaign. The ad showed a close-up photo of Colin's face with the phrase "Believe in something. Even if it means sacrificing everything." Nike realized what a sacrifice Colin had made to stand for social justice. Many people rejoiced over the new ad, happy that such a big company recognized the important work Colin Kaepernick was doing for Black people.

But others were angry. There were still many people in the United States who felt what Colin started was disrespectful to American soldiers, the American flag, and the American people. Colin's critics were very unhappy with Nike for supporting the sports star. They took videos of themselves burning all of their Nike gear and uploaded the footage to social media in protest.

Even though there were negative reactions to the Nike campaign, organizations continued to honor Colin for taking a stand for social justice.

CHAPTER 5
Know Your Rights

The NFL worked hard to get Colin Kaepernick's complaint against them dismissed. But, by now, it had been a whole year and no NFL team had hired Colin to play for them. On August 30, 2018, an arbitrator—or person appointed to settle a dispute—had decided Colin *did* have enough evidence to support his claims that the NFL was blackballing him. The arbitrator denied the NFL's request to dismiss Colin's complaint.

Colin and the NFL battled it out away from the cameras and the media for several months. On February 15, 2019, the two sides reached a secret agreement. Although Colin still hadn't been recruited by a team, the NFL agreed to pay him an unknown amount of money to make up for all the time he missed off the field.

After Colin's complaint was settled with the NFL, he concentrated on his activism full time. He convinced Nike to remove the original thirteen-starred American flag on one of its shoes. This flag symbolizes a time when the enslavement of Black people was legal. Colin didn't think this sent a good message to customers.

Colin was happy to make a difference in his community. But his love of the game never stopped. In August 2019, Colin tweeted out a message to the NFL and included a video of himself working out. He let the NFL teams know he was ready to get back on the field. But none of the NFL owners reached out.

Finally, on November 12, 2019, the NFL announced they would set up a private workout session for Colin at the Atlanta Falcons practice facility the following week. They invited coaches from thirty-two teams to observe Colin's skills during his workout.

But the NFL had rules for Colin. Among other things, he was only given two hours to confirm or decline the invitation to attend. He would not be allowed to bring his own camera crew. Colin didn't fully trust the arrangement. Shortly before start time, Colin announced he was moving the workout to a high-school one hour away from the Falcons facility. Only eight NFL teams made the trip to watch Colin play, but that was fine with him. He was still able to show that he had the arm and speed to be a serious contender in the NFL.

Today, Colin Kaepernick continues to fight for the justice of Black and Brown people. His Know Your Rights Camp has expanded to several major cities all over the United States, including Miami, Baltimore, and Atlanta. The camp now includes a legal defense fund that helps Black and Brown protesters who are arrested or are the victims of police brutality.

In June 2020, soon after yet another Black man, George Floyd, was videotaped being murdered by a police officer, the NFL commissioner Roger Goodell admitted in an interview that he and the NFL were wrong for silencing their players for protesting police brutality. In August 2020, in another interview, Roger said, "I wish we had listened earlier, Kaep, to what you were kneeling about and what you were trying to bring attention to."

In 2016, Colin Kaepernick kneeled on the football field to bring attention to police brutality against Black people. Today, he stands up for justice.

Timeline of Colin Kaepernick's Life

1987 — Colin Kaepernick is born on November 3

— Adopted by the Kaepernick family

1991 — Moves to California with his family

2006 — Attends the University of Nevada, Reno, and begins
playing football one year later

2011 — Drafted into the NFL by the San Francisco 49ers

2016 — Begins kneeling during the national anthem to
protest police brutality

— Other NFL players join Colin's protest, which sparks a
nationwide debate

— Starts the Know Your Rights Camp so children will be
informed when interacting with police officers

2017 — Opts out of his contract with the San Francisco 49ers
and becomes a free agent

— Files a complaint against the NFL owners for working
together to keep him from playing in the NFL

2020 — Starts a defense fund to help Black activists when
they are arrested or are victims of police brutality

Timeline of the World

1987	Aretha Franklin becomes the first female musician inducted into the Rock & Roll Hall of Fame
1991	Boris Yeltsin wins Russia's first presidential election
2006	Pluto is downgraded from a planet to a dwarf planet
2011	The Egyptian Revolution begins, as citizens protest against government corruption and poverty
2017	Donald Trump is inaugurated on January 20 as president of the United States of America
2018	Biracial American actress Meghan Markle marries Prince Harry, Duke of Sussex
2020	The novel coronavirus disease COVID-19 spreads all over the world, sickening and killing millions of people
2021	Kamala Harris is sworn in as the first female vice president of the United States of America

Bibliography

*Books for young readers

Bunton, Kristie. *Having Their Say: Athletes and Entertainers and the Ethics of Speaking Out*. Jefferson, NC: McFarland & Company Inc., 2021.

*Easton, Emily, and Ziyue Chen. *Enough! 20+ Protesters Who Changed America*. Updated edition. New York: Dragonfly Books, 2021

Railton, Ben. *Of Thee I Sing: The Contested History of American Patriotism*. Lanham, MD: Rowman & Littlefield, 2021.

*Reynolds, Jason, and Ibram X. Kendi. *Stamped: Racism, Antiracism, and You*. New York: Little, Brown Books for Young Readers, 2020.

*Reynolds, Jason, Ibram X. Kendi, Sonja Cherry-Paul, and Rachelle Baker. ***Stamped (For Kids): Racism, Antiracism, and You.*** New York: Little, Brown Books for Young Readers, 2021.

*Rhodes, Jewell Parker. ***Ghost Boys***. New York: Little, Brown Books for Young Readers, 2018.

*Tyner, Artika R. ***Black Lives Matter: From Hashtag to the Streets***. The Fight for Black Rights. Minneapolis, MN: Lerner Publications, 2021.

*Walker, Hubert. ***Colin Kaepernick: Football Star***. Biggest Names in Sports. Mendota Heights, MN: Focus Readers, 2021.

Zirin, Dave. ***The Kaepernick Effect: Taking a Knee, Changing the World***. New York: The New Press, 2021.

YOUR HEADQUARTERS FOR HISTORY